Bugs Are Beautiful!

A+ books

DAZZLING
Dragonflies

by Catherine Ipcizade

Consultant:
Laura Jesse
Director, Plant and Insect Diagnostic Clinic
Iowa State University Extension
Ames, Iowa

• • •

CAPSTONE PRESS
a capstone imprint

A+ Books are published by Capstone Press
1710 Roe Crest Drive, North Mankato, Minnesota 56003
www.mycapstone.com

Library of Congress Cataloging-in-Publication Data
Names: Ipcizade, Catherine, author.
Title: Dazzling dragonflies / by Catherine Ipcizade.
Description: North Mankato, Minnesota : Capstone Press, [2017] |
Series: Bugs are beautiful! | Audience: Ages 4-8. | Audience: K to grade 3. | Includes bibliographical references and index.
Identifiers: LCCN 2016032403| ISBN 9781515744986 (library binding) | ISBN 9781515745020 (pbk.) | ISBN 9781515745143 (eBook PDF)
Subjects: LCSH: Dragonflies—Juvenile literature.
Classification: LCC QL520 .I66 2017 | DDC 595.7/33—dc23
LC record available at https://lccn.loc.gov/2016032403

Editorial Credits
Editor, Abby Colich; Designer, Bobbie Nuytten; Media Researcher, Jo Miller; Production Specialist, Tori Abraham

Photo Credits
Alamy: Wong Hock weng, 23; Dreamstime: 57920346, 30 (all); Minden Pictures: John Abbott, 18, NPL/Paul Harcourt Davies, 21; Nature Picture Library: Aflo, 22; Science Source: B.G. Thomson, 28; Shutterstock: Abeselom Zerit, 1, David Byron Keener, 19, Dennis van de Water, 24, Gerald A. DeBoer, 9, Jan-Nor Photography, 5 (bottom left), Jayne Gulbrand, 8, Judith Lienert, 11, 17, kesipun, 4, KPL, 5 (top), kurt_G, 10, Paul Reeves Photography, 14, 15, 27, paulrommer, 5 (bottom right), Peter Eggermann, 6, 7, Puwadol Jaturawutthichai, map (throughout), Richard A McMillin, cover, 13, RODINA OLENA, back cover (background), SDeming, 26, Simon_g, 25, Yongkiet Jitwattanatam, 16, Yuval Heifman, 12, SuperStock: Juniors, 20; UIG via Getty Images: Auscape/Contributor, 29

Note to Parents, Teachers, and Librarians

This Bugs Are Beautiful book uses full-color photographs and a nonfiction format to introduce the concept of dragonflies. Bugs Are Beautiful is designed to be read aloud to a pre-reader or to be read independently by an early reader. Photographs help listeners and early readers understand the text and concepts discussed. The book encourages further learning by including the following sections: Table of Contents, Glossary, Read More, Internet Sites, Critical Thinking Using the Common Core, and Index. Early readers may need assistance using these features.

Printed in the United States   4932

Table of Contents

Dragonflies Are **Dazzling!**

Zoom! A dragonfly flutters by. Its two pairs of wings move quickly. Its huge eyes search for food. The dragonfly spots a bug. Gulp! It swallows its prey.

Dragonflies can be bright colors. Some have cool spots or patterns. These insects will dazzle you!

Broad-Bodied **Chaser**

male

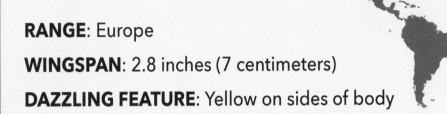

RANGE: Europe

WINGSPAN: 2.8 inches (7 centimeters)

DAZZLING FEATURE: Yellow on sides of body

Chomp! The broad-bodied chaser eats a bug. Then it flies back to its perch. This dragonfly likes to hang out in one spot. It waits there for the next bug.

This dragonfly's body is thick and flat. A male's body is light blue. A female's body is yellow or brown. Both have bright yellow on their sides.

female

Calico Pennant

male

RANGE: United States and Canada

WINGSPAN: 2.4 inches (6 cm)

DAZZLING FEATURE: Heart-shaped spots

What shapes are on the calico pennant's back? Hearts! Red hearts run down a male's back. A female has yellow hearts on her back. These dragonflies have black bodies. Colorful spots mark their wings.

female

Crimson Marsh Glider

RANGE: Asia

LENGTH: 1.2 inches (3 cm)

DAZZLING COLOR: Bright pink

Wow! The male crimson marsh glider stands out. His body is bright pink! His face is red. A female is gold or brown. Check out their wings. They are transparent. Colored veins run through them.

veins

Flame Skimmer

RANGE: Parts of the United States and Mexico

WINGSPAN: 1.8 inches (4.5 cm)

DAZZLING COLOR: Bright orange

Can you guess what color the flame skimmer is? Males are bright orange, just like flames. Females are brown. Their wings are transparent with brown edges.

Flame skimmers like it hot. They live where it's warm. Some even live near hot springs.

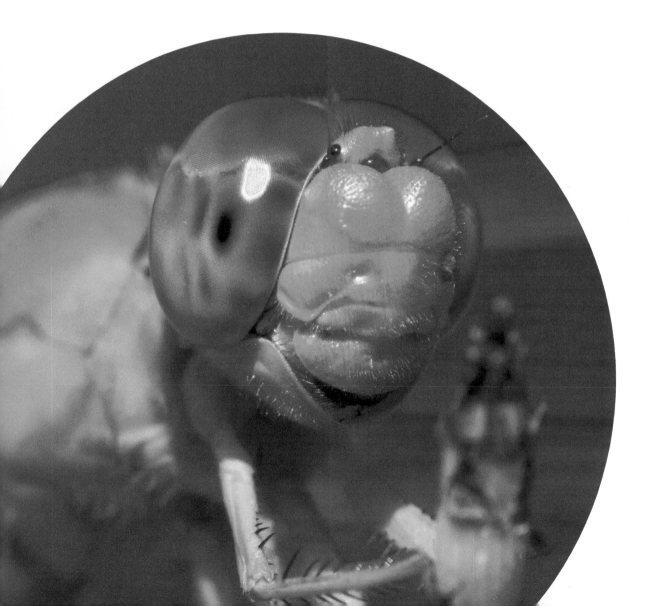

Green **Darner**

RANGE: North America

WINGSPAN: 3.2 inches (8 cm)

DAZZLING FEATURE: Target
   mark on head

Zoom! Green darners are fast. They fly up to 35 miles (56 kilometers) per hour. At the end of summer, they fly south. Huge swarms travel together. Then they mate. Some of the offspring fly north in spring.

See the mark on the top of its head? The mark looks like a target.

Fulvous Forest Skimmer

female

Those are some bold wings! The fulvous forest skimmer's wings are mostly colored. Only the tips are transparent. Males are red with brown heads. Females are rust colored. This dragonfly lives in forests. It sticks to areas that are moist. Skimmers do a lot of hunting. They fly around looking for food.

RANGE: India

WINGSPAN: 2.4 inches (6 cm)

DAZZLING FEATURE: Colored wings

male

Halloween Pennant

RANGE: United States and Canada

WINGSPAN: 2.4 inches (6 cm)

DAZZLING COLORS: Yellow-orange and black or brown

Boo! The Halloween pennant is yellow-orange and black or brown. It perches on top of bushes or tall grass. Whoosh! Wind blows the plant. The dragonfly moves with it. The insect looks like a pennant, or flag, as it sways. This dragonfly is strong. It can fly in heavy wind and rain.

RANGE: Europe

WINGSPAN: 2.4 inches (6 cm)

DAZZLING COLORS: Red and yellow

What's this dragonfly's mouth full of? Bugs! The ruddy darter can hold eight fruit flies in its mouth at once. Ruddy darters like water with lots of plants. Larvae spend a year under water. Adults are yellow. Males turn red as they age.

Scarlet Dwarf

male

RANGE: Asia

WINGSPAN: 0.8 inch (2 cm)

DAZZLING SKILL: Handstands

What's that dragonfly doing? A handstand!
It's a hot day. The scarlet dwarf lifts its tail end
toward the sky. The rest of its body stays cool.

This dragonfly is the world's smallest. It's about
the size of your fingertip. The male's tiny body is
red. A female is white, yellow, and brown.

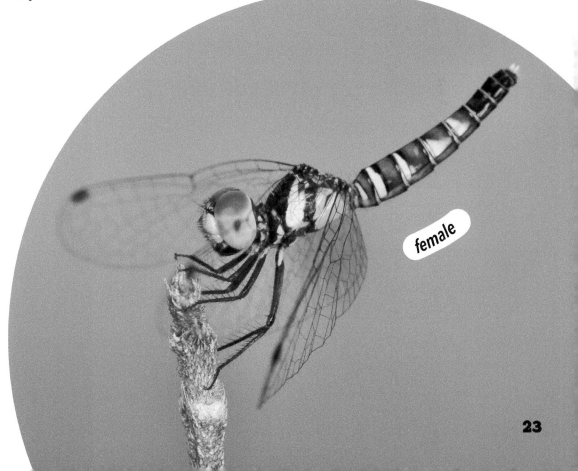

female

Phantom Flutterer

RANGE: Africa, Middle East

LENGTH: 1.4 inches (3.6 cm)

DAZZLING FEATURE: Bright
colors on wings

Ooh! Can you see those bright colors? A phantom flutterer sports purple, blue, or red on its wings. Its body is blue. The bright colors shine in the light. Flutterers get their name because they fly like butterflies.

Twelve-Spotted Skimmer

female

RANGE: United States and Canada

WINGSPAN: 4 inches (10.2 cm)

DAZZLING FEATURE: Spots on wings

Can you count the spots on this dragonfly? The twelve-spotted skimmer has three dark spots on each wing. That's 12 spots. A male has 10 more spots that are white.

A male watches over his territory. Another male comes near. They fly in loops around each other. One male flies away, confused. The other male wins the territory.

male

Wandering Percher

What's that flash of red? It's a male wandering percher. A female wandering percher dips her tail end into the water. She is laying eggs. The male holds onto her. This keeps other males away.

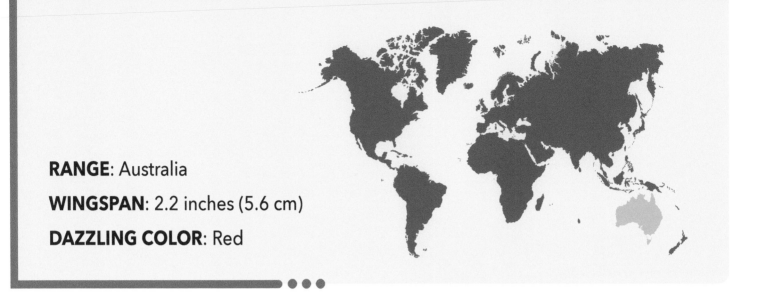

RANGE: Australia

WINGSPAN: 2.2 inches (5.6 cm)

DAZZLING COLOR: Red

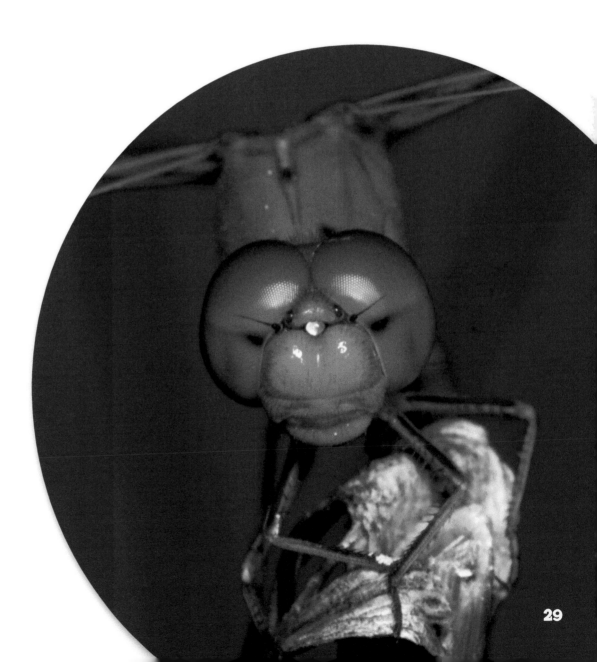

Life Cycle of a Dragonfly

1 Dragonflies begin life as eggs.

2 A larva, or nymph, hatches from an egg.

3 A nymph molts as it grows into an adult.

4 adult dragonfly

Glossary

feature (FEE-chur)—an important part or quality of something

flutter (FLUHT-ur)—to wave or flap quickly

hot spring (HOT SPRING)—a place where warm water comes out of the ground

larva (LAR-vuh)—an insect at a stage of development between egg and adult

mate (MATE)—to join together to produce young

molt (MOLT)—to shed the hard outer covering while growing

offspring (AWF-spring)—the young of a person, animal, or plant

perch (PURCH)—a high place where a bird or insect can rest and view its surroundings

prey (PRAY)—an animal hunted by another animal for food

range (RAYNJ)—an area where an animal mostly lives

swarm (SWARM)—to gather or fly close together in a large group

territory (TARE-uh-tore-ee)—an area of land that an animal claims as its own to live in

transparent (transs-PAIR-uhnt)—easily seen through

vein (VAYN)—small, stiff tube that helps give shape to a bug's wings

Read More

Hansen, Grace. *Becoming a Dragonfly*. Changing Animals. Minneapolis: ABDO Kids, 2016.

Nelson, Robin. *Darting Dragonflies*. Backyard Critters. Minneapolis: Lerner, 2016.

Rissman, Rebecca. *Dragonflies*. Creepy Critters. Chicago: Raintree, 2013.

Internet Sites

FactHound offers a safe, fun way to find Internet sites related to this book.
All of the sites on FactHound have been researched by our staff.

Here's all you do:

Visit *www.facthound.com*

Type in this code: 9781515744986

 Check out projects, games and lots more at
www.capstonekids.com

Critical Thinking Using the Common Core

1. How many pairs of wings does a dragonfly have? (Key Ideas and Details)

2. Page 13 says some flame skimmers live near hot springs. Use the glossary on page 31 to define hot spring. (Craft and Structure)

3. Choose two dragonflies that are discussed in the book. How are they alike? How are they different? (Integration of Knowledge and Ideas)

Index